THE EUREK… MOMENT

Scientist profile

Name: Charles Robert Darwin

Date of birth: 12th February, 1809

Date of death: 19th April, 1882

Education: University of Edinburgh
Christ's College, Cambridge

Major achievements:

- Voyaging on the *Beagle*
- Visiting the Galapagos islands and studying its strange creatures
- Developing the theory of evolution by natural selection
- Writing bestselling science books that changed the world
- Growing a very impressive beard

First published in the UK in 2019
by The Salariya Book Company Ltd.
This edition published in the UK in 2024 by Hatch Press,
an imprint of Bonnier Book UK
4th Floor, Victoria House
Bloomsbury Square, London WC1B 4DA
Owned by Bonnier Books
Sveavägen 56, Stockholm, Sweden
www.bonnierbooks.co.uk

1 3 5 7 9 10 8 6 4 2

ISBN 978-1-80078-847-3

Printed in the United Kingdom

THE EUREKA! MOMENT

Charles Darwin & Evolution

Written by
Ian Graham

Illustrated by
Annaliese Stoney

Hatch

Introduction

28th May, 1876

"My feet sank into jet black sand as if I had stepped onto another planet. The heat was almost unbearable as if the fires of Hell were burning beneath my boots. Beyond the shore, the rock was as hard as iron, and black as the sand. Huge lizards as ugly as I have ever seen scurried around me as I walked. That night, I dined on tortoise—meat cooked over an open fire under the stars. Imagine that. The tortoise was a giant creature that could carry a man on its back with ease. And the birds. I scarcely noticed the birds at first, flocks of them, little brown birds. I didn't know it at the time, but these tiny birds would change my life and cause a revolution in biology. I almost missed their meaning. Their importance did not come to me until after I had left this alien place. It was only when I thought about them afterwards that I noticed something odd about them. And it changed everything." Charles Darwin paused to collect his thoughts.

His son, Francis, was sitting by him. He said, "The seashore was actually made of furnace-hot, black sand?"

"Yes," said Charles. "It was the islands, you see. The Galapagos Islands. They're made of lava—black volcanic rock. And they lie on the equator, so the Sun beats down on the bare rock without mercy. It's a wonder that anything can live there."

"They sound remarkable."

Darwin went on. “Indeed they are. And the voyage to reach such remote islands was just as memorable. I saw whales the size of steam trains leaping from the ocean, and I was shaken to the bone by an earthquake that ruined a city. I explored places that few people in this great land have ever set foot on, or ever will. And to do this and more, I sailed around the world, something that little more than a handful of Englishmen have ever done.”

He seemed lost in thought for a few moments. Then he said, “When I was a young man, my life seemed mapped out for me. I was sent to university to be a doctor, as my father had been, but I was more interested in studying the natural world. No one could have imagined how it would all play out.”

“Thank goodness you didn’t become a doctor. You might never have unravelled the mystery of evolution.”

"It's hard to believe now, but my work caused such outrage, such anger," said Charles, "that there were times when I feared my friends and fellow scientists might cast me into the wilderness and never speak to me again."

"It's a great adventure," said Francis. "More people should know about it."

Charles thought about this and then he said, "I would love to have read something written by my grandfather about what he thought and did, and how he worked. So, I think you're right, Francis. The time has come for me to set down my story..."

Chapter 1

1817

I've been a collector all my life. Even as a little boy of eight or nine years old at school in Shrewsbury, I collected all sorts of things – eggs, rocks, shells, coins. I had a passion for it that none of my brothers or sisters shared.

I did not do well at school. I was treated like a below-average student, and so I was quite a disappointment to my father. I remember him saying to me one day, "You care for nothing but shooting, dogs, and rat-catching, and you will be a disgrace to yourself and all your family." I thought it quite harsh from someone who was normally the kindest father a son could wish for. Perhaps he was trying to shock me into changing my ways for the better.

Darwin's family

Charles Darwin and his wife, Emma, had ten children: six boys and four girls. Two of their children (Mary Eleanor and Charles Waring) died as babies and a third child (Anne Elizabeth) died at the age of ten. This number of child deaths in a family of ten was normal at that time. Three of Darwin's children (George, Francis and Horace) became important scientists and engineers.

I remember reading a book called *Wonders of the World*. It made me want to travel to far-away countries so that I could see the marvels of nature for myself. As I turned 16, I was doing so badly at school that my father despaired. He took me out of school and said, "My boy, to save you from yourself I have decided that you are to go to Edinburgh University to study medicine, as I did. You are to follow in my footsteps as a doctor. I am certain it will be the making of you."

During the summer before I left for Edinburgh, I visited some of the poor and needy of Shrewsbury and wrote notes on their illnesses for my father. My keen interest in this work made him think that I would make a good physician.

Sadly, it soon became clear that I had no more interest in medicine than in my classes at school. Most of the time I found the study of medicine dull. When it wasn't dull, it was disgusting. Instead, I spent a great deal of my time with people who

Sherlock Holmes

Darwin studied medicine at the University of Edinburgh Medical School, although he didn't complete his course. One of the school's lecturers, Joseph Bell, was famous for his ability to notice symptoms in his patients that others missed. These clues might tell him what a patient's job was or where a patient had travelled recently. One of Bell's students went on to write stories about a fictional detective with the same skills. The student was Arthur Conan Doyle and he called his detective Sherlock Holmes.

knew a lot about geology, zoology, botany and other natural sciences. I studied creatures in rock pools on the seashore and collected fish by going out in boats with fishermen.

Somehow my father, my poor father, heard about my lack of interest in medicine, so he set about saving me from a wasted life for a second time. With great disappointment, he said, "It seems that you are not to be a doctor after all. Then you must be a clergyman. You are headed for the church, my boy."

To become a country parson, I first needed a degree from an English university. So, after two years in Edinburgh, I began a new course of study at Cambridge University.

I am not, and never have been, a clergyman. I wasted my time at Cambridge just as I had wasted my time at Edinburgh. Once again, I was more interested in nature. I studied botany and went on field trips to see all manner of rocks, plants and

NO INTERESTING BEETLES HERE TODAY.
AT LAST, SOMETHING WORTH COLLECTING.
TWO MORE BEAUTIES FOR MY COLLECTION.
I MUST HAVE YOU, BUT HOW TO PICK YOU UP.

THERE IS ALWAYS AN ANSWER.
GOT YOU ALL!
UGH! INFERNAL CREATURE! MY TONGUE IS ON FIRE!

animals. It was while I was at Cambridge that I began collecting beetles.

At Cambridge I met the man who would change the course of my life in a most surprising way. He was professor John Stevens Henslow. He had a great knowledge of every branch of science. I got to know him well and went on long walks with him. I was known as 'the man who walks with Henslow'. I think he saw some promise in me. At long last, here was someone who thought that I might not be simply lazy.

In August 1831, I returned home from a field trip to North Wales to find a letter from Henslow waiting for me. He had been asked to join a naval survey voyage as the expedition's naturalist. The voyage was to last two years. It proved to be too long for Henslow's wife, who persuaded him to give up his place. He said it would be terrible if this rare chance was lost, so it was important that another naturalist should be found to take his place. The ship, HMS *Beagle*, was to sail a month later, so time was short. To my amazement, Henslow suggested that I should go instead of him. There were better naturalists, but he said that my long experience of collecting specimens from nature made me the perfect choice.

A few days later I sent my reply to Henslow, but it was not the news he wanted. When I talked to my father about the offer, he was against me going. He said, "This useless voyage will delay you settling down for another two years. It will be yet another pointless change of profession, since you have already given up your studies to be a doctor and a clergyman."

He also felt that my tiny cabin in a naval vessel would be uncomfortable and, as others had already turned down the chance to go, there must be something wrong with the ship or the expedition that was unknown to me. He was so certain he was right that he said, "If you can find any man of common sense who tells you to go, I will agree to it." And so, I told Henslow that I could not go.

The next day I visited my uncle, Josiah Wedgwood, at his Staffordshire home. When I told him what had happened, he took me home to Shrewsbury and told my father he thought I should take my place on the expedition. He thought it a great opportunity for a young man. My father always thought Josiah to be a very sensible man with good judgement, so he changed his mind and gave me his support. He said, "I promise to give you all the help I can."

This was music to my ears, because my place on the ship was unpaid, so my father would have to foot the bill for all my expenses during the voyage. He agreed to do this, so I immediately hurried to London to meet the *Beagle*'s captain, Robert FitzRoy.

Chapter summary:

- Charles Darwin is a poor student at school and fails to complete his university studies as either a doctor or a clergyman.
- Whilst at university, he discovers a passion for nature.
- He meets professor John Stevens Henslow, who suggests that he take his place as naturalist on an expedition aboard the HMS *Beagle*. Darwin jumps at the chance.

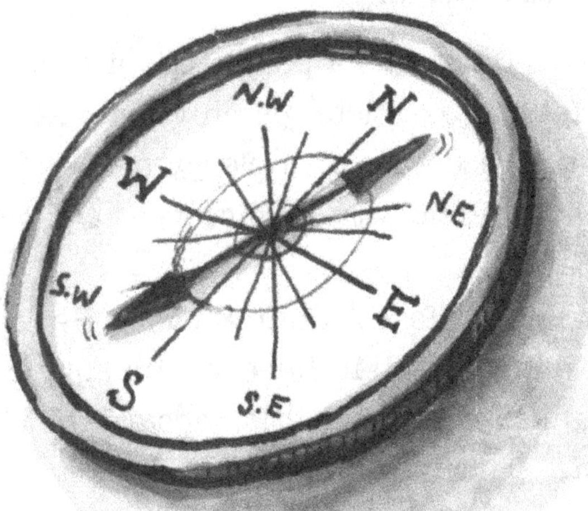
N.W
N
W
N.E
S.W
E
S
S.E

Chapter 2

1891

I arrived at the Devonport naval dockyard on Monday, 24th October, 1831. The rest of October and November flew by in a blur of preparations to leave. Carpenters and painters readied the *Beagle*, while officers stowed their equipment and belongings, and the crew loaded supplies. I was to share Captain FitzRoy's cabin on the ship, so my living space was small and not in the least private. There was not one inch of wasted space anywhere in the ship.

HMS *Beagle*

The *Beagle* was a two-masted sailing ship, built for the Royal Navy as a warship meant for battles at sea. She was launched in 1820 and then, in 1825, converted to a survey vessel by adding a third mast and removing some of her guns. She was one of the first ships to be fitted with lightning conductors to protect her from lightning strikes. In 1845, after two long survey voyages, she was used as a watch vessel, stationed on the coast to look out for smugglers. She was broken up in 1870.

My scientific work began even before we set sail. I was given the job of taking air pressure readings from the ship's barometers every morning. Changes in air pressure are related to the weather. High pressure brings fair weather and light winds. Low pressure is a sign of poor weather, like rain and stronger winds. Rapidly falling air pressure can be the first clue that a storm is heading our way. It was during this time that I made my first great discovery. There are many wrong ways to get into a hammock, and only one right way! After a number of fruitless attempts, I was shown the correct method. You simply sit in the middle of the hammock and twist around to bring your head and feet to the right positions.

Our departure was delayed for several days by poor weather. Finally, on the 10th December, we set sail. It was a joy to see the ship's crew come to life as a working machine, every man knowing his place and springing into action at the commands shouted by the officers on the deck. My joy did not last long. By the evening we found ourselves in the teeth of a strong gale and stormy sea that made the ship pitch up and down alarmingly. I felt horribly seasick. The next morning there was no sign of the storm weakening, so we turned back to land. Bad weather kept us in port another ten days. When we tried to leave again, we were driven back to harbour by more bad weather. Our epic voyage finally began on 27th December. Even though the weather was now fair, I suffered from seasickness again. I hardly left my hammock for more than a week before the illness left me. When I could go out on deck and take in the view, I was amazed by the brightness of the blue colour in the sea. And the nights! My goodness, the nights. The tropical night sky is so clear and dark, and the stars shine so bright as I have never seen before.

Robert FitzRoy

The *Beagle*'s captain, Robert FitzRoy (1805–1865), was sent to naval training college at the age of 12. He worked his way up through the ranks until he was given command of the *Beagle* at the age of only 23. The voyage he undertook with Charles Darwin made him famous, especially after he wrote a book about it. He was elected as a Member of Parliament in 1841 and then became the governor of New Zealand. On his return to Britain, he was soon heading a new organisation that collected weather information at sea. He used this information to predict the weather to come. He called his predictions weather forecasts.

I must tell you something startling that I discovered about the reason for my invitation to join the expedition. Before FitzRoy took command of the *Beagle*, the ship's captain was a man called Pringle Stokes. He commanded the *Beagle* on her first great voyage to survey the coast of Patagonia and Tierra del Fuego in South America. The difficulties of the voyage made Captain Stokes unwell. He fell into a great depression and locked himself in his cabin for two weeks. In the end, the poor man shot himself. He was replaced by Captain FitzRoy. Keen to avoid a similar fate on the *Beagle*'s next voyage to the same waters, FitzRoy decided to take a companion, the expedition's naturalist. On discovering this, I joked that my job was to keep the captain sane so that he might survive the voyage! This thought would return to haunt me, but more of that later.

We sailed south-west across the Atlantic Ocean,

calling in at islands on the way to take on food and water. I collected specimens from the ocean by means of a net trailed in the water behind the ship. This provided the answer to something that had puzzled me. The *Beagle* was sometimes accompanied by large sea creatures, among them porpoises, whales and great fish. As I watched porpoises leaping through white-topped waves near the ship, I wondered aloud, "How do these creatures survive? What do they eat?"

"Fish," came the reply, as if the question was silly. The ship's surgeon, Robert MacCormick, stood alongside me.

"But what do the fish feed on in these deep clear waters far from the coast? I asked. Aside from creatures of such great size, the ocean water seems quite lifeless."

MacCormick shrugged his shoulders and went about his business. My net soon gave me the answer. It brought up great numbers of very small animals, many of them so small that they were only visible under a microscope. It must be these that the larger creatures feed upon. I told the sailor who helped me pull the net onboard, "There is a whole chain of life in the ocean, from the tiniest creature to the biggest, each feeding upon the next."

My collection of specimens quickly grew, especially when we visited islands and went ashore. There were soon so many specimens that I worried no one in England would have the time or interest to look at them all. My first footstep on a tropical shore was at St Jago in the Cape Verd islands. It was an experience I'll never forget. On my return to the ship I told Captain FitzRoy, "I was like a blind man given fresh eyes, so overcome was I by the sight of so many new plants, insects and animals."

When we crossed the equator in February, those of us who were making the crossing for

Changing names

The names of some islands and countries have changed over the centuries, often as a result of wars or being conquered by other countries. During his voyage, Darwin wrote in his diary about visiting an island called St Jago in the Cape Verd islands, but you won't find St Jago on a map today. It is now known as Santiago in the Cape Verde islands.

the first time knew that an uncomfortable fate awaited us. It is a tradition in the navy that a sailor's first crossing of the equator should be something he never forgets. Myself and about 30 others were kept below deck while noisy preparations went on above us. I was the first

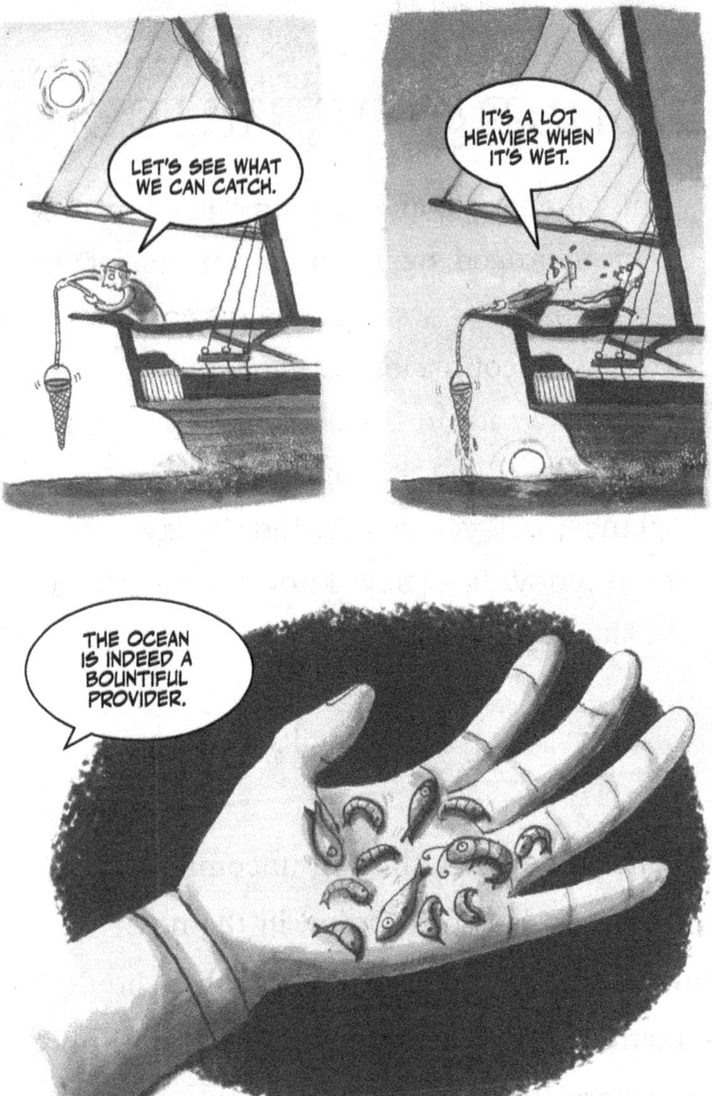
LET'S SEE WHAT WE CAN CATCH.
IT'S A LOT HEAVIER WHEN IT'S WET.
THE OCEAN IS INDEED A BOUNTIFUL PROVIDER.

NEW SPECIMENS FOR MY COLLECTION.
WHAT WONDERFUL CREATURES.
IT'S IMPORTANT TO RECORD DETAILS OF ALL THE CREATURES.
THE WATER IS TEEMING WITH CREATURES TOO SMALL TO SEE.

to be led back up on deck, blindfolded. Suddenly, there was a great noise all around me and I was struck by buckets of water from all sides. I was held still while my face was covered with soap and scraped clean as if I was being shaven, after which I was pushed into a bath of water. The whole ceremony was overseen by Neptune, God of the Sea – in reality a heavily disguised sailor. Once this strange tradition was over, we continued on our way, driven on by the Trade Wind.

We reached the coast of Brazil at the end of February, two months after leaving England. For a naturalist, the tropical vegetation was an amazing sight. I went ashore and walked through the forest collecting flowers and insects, but mainly taking in the extraordinary beauty of the scenery.

We continued south to Rio de Janeiro and Montevideo. I took every chance to explore the land while the *Beagle* went about its survey work at sea. The heat was difficult to bear, at times reaching as much as 96 degrees. On one return to the ship, I learned that three of our ship-mates had died of fevers. Assistant surgeon Bynoe saw my shock and said, "Death is common on these long voyages. Lives are often lost through disease and accident. You must prepare yourself for more. All hands know when they sign up for service that they might never see their homes again."

One night, nature showed us an extraordinary sight. While lightning flashed through the tar-black sky, the tops of our masts and the ends of the yards glowed brightly due to an effect known as St Elmo's fire. At the same time, looking over the ship's rail, I could see penguins racing through the water, leaving glowing trails behind them.

Further south in Patagonia, I was treated to a dinner unlike any ever enjoyed in England –

ostrich dumplings and armadillo. To my great surprise, the ostrich meat tasted more like beef than that of a bird and the armadillo meat tasted like duck.

My specimen collection continued to grow. Not only did I shoot many birds and catch lots of snakes, but I found a number of fossil bones. They included a large skull and the jaw bone of an animal I knew to be a Megatherium, a sloth the size of an elephant.

Just before Christmas 1832, we made the coast of Tierra del Fuego for the first time. Soon after, Cape Horn came into view. We had long left behind the tropical forests teeming with life. Bitter winds blew dark clouds over the jagged, snow-covered crags of the cape. The gales whipped the sea until it was foaming violently. While the *Beagle* spent the next year sailing up and down the coast to Brazil and back, checking and re-checking its map-making, I went ashore and explored the land.

Mysterious lights

When ships like the *Beagle* sailed through thunderstorms, sailors sometimes saw a bright blue or violet glow at the tops of the masts and the tips of the yardarms. It's caused by the electricity produced by the storm, the same electricity that causes lightning. The glow in the sea that Darwin saw was different. It was caused by tiny plants called algae that glowed when penguins swam through the water and disturbed them. Light produced by living things is called bioluminescence.

The *Beagle* was our home, our workplace and our protection from the elements. It was vital to keep the ship in a good state of repair, for without it we were lost. The one part of it that lay beyond the crew's reach was the hull below the water-line. Captain FitzRoy decided that it should be checked before we sailed into the Pacific Ocean. At the mouth of the Santa Cruz river, the captain found a suitable shore for his purpose. The crew sailed the ship onto the beach so that its hull could be checked at low tide. It was in good condition apart from several feet of her false keel that had been knocked off. Repairs were quickly made and the ship was floated off the beach at the next high tide.

The Santa Cruz, a large river, had been explored during the *Beagle*'s last voyage under Captain Stokes, but a lack of food and other items meant that the expedition had to be cut short. The upper part of the river remained unknown, so Captain FitzRoy now took three whale boats and 25 men upstream to explore. Miraculously, one of the crew found a boat hook that had been lost there seven years earlier. On the shore, we found

Mapping the oceans

To stay safe at sea, sailors need to know the positions of islands, coastlines and dangerous rocks, so they need maps. The Hydrographic Office in Britain sent ships all over the world to make maps. HMS *Beagle* was one of these ships.

the footprints of horses and the remains of fires – signs of the local peoples who lived along the river. And we saw herds of up to 500 guanaco, animals similar to camels standing about three feet tall. The crew shot ten of these strange animals for food. I also shot a condor, a bird with a vast wingspan of some eight and a half feet.

We returned to Cape Horn in June, 1834, and this time we passed through the Strait of

Magellan to the Pacific Ocean. In July, we reached Valparaiso in Chile, which was to be my home for the next few months while the *Beagle* surveyed the coast. I made a remarkable discovery there. In the foothills of the Andes mountains, I found land that was covered with seashells, but this land was no seashore. It was 1,300 feet above the sea. Unlikely as it may seem, I thought the land must once have been under the sea and had been lifted to its present position. Unimaginable forces must have been at play to cause such a thing to happen. But what forces? How could it happen? I had my answer a few months later.

While I was walking with my servant, Syms Covington, near Valdivia in southern Chile, I lay down in a wood near the coast to catch my breath when I thought I felt a movement in the ground below me. Syms felt it too. He said, "Sir? Do my senses deceive me? Is the ground moving?"

Before I could answer, there was no mistaking it. The ground was certainly moving. The rocking and shaking went on for two minutes. I found that I could stand up, but the motion of the ground made me dizzy. I looked around and shouted to Syms, "It's an earthquake. Look at the trees. They're swaying."

When the shaking passed, we walked into the town of Valdivia. The wooden houses there showed little damage. I asked one man what had happened. He said, "The houses were violently shaken and creaked a lot." He showed me that some of the nails that held his home together had been partly pushed out by the quake. There was horror and fear in the faces of the people.

When I returned to the *Beagle* I told Captain FitzRoy, "The world shuddered and shook beneath our feet like a crust floating over a fluid."

We sailed 200 miles up the coast to the Bay of Concepcion where we found an awful sight. The coast was covered with timber and furniture as if a thousand great ships had been wrecked. Local people told us that 70 villages had been destroyed by the earthquake and a great wave from the sea that followed it. Huge slabs of rock had been thrown up onto the shore and cracks a yard wide had opened up in the ground. The great city of Concepcion itself looked like an ancient ruin. Row after row of houses had been reduced to heaps of rubble. Earthquakes were so common here that the people ran from their homes at the first tremble of the ground. Such a habit must surely have saved many lives.

Mr Rous, the English Consul in Concepcion, told me, "At the first motion I ran out, but I reached only the middle of my little courtyard when one side of my house came thundering down. The shaking of the ground was so bad that I was unable to stand upright and had to crawl upon my hands and knees. Then the other side of my house fell. Its great wooden beams fell close by my head as they tumbled down around me. The cloud of dust thrown up was so thick that the sky darkened."

Meanwhile people on the shore saw a large wave travelling towards them. They ran for high ground to save themselves. When the wave broke on the shore, it reached a height of 23 feet above high tide. It pushed a gun carriage weighing four tons out of position by 15 feet. The most surprising sight of all was a fine sailing ship that had been carried 200 yards inland and now sat in the middle of the town. The length of the coast affected was 400 miles.

The earthquake was one of the worst to strike Chile that the country's people could remember. It lifted the land around the Bay of Concepcion two or three feet. On the nearby island of Santa Maria, Captain FitzRoy found beds of terribly foul-smelling, rotting mussels as much as ten feet above the water. Local people told him that before the earthquake they used to dive for these shellfish. Here were the forces that could raise whole islands and lift the seabed out of the water, leaving seashells high and dry.

During my time ashore in Chile an event occurred on the *Beagle* that threatened to change everything that followed. It might have cut the expedition short before we reached our next destination, the Galapagos Islands. If this had indeed been our fate, then I would never have set foot on those magical islands. The theory of evolution by natural selection would have been the work of others, not Charles Darwin. What a different life I might have had.

When I returned to the ship, the first officer, John Wickham, told me the sorry tale. "Captain FitzRoy was worried that he might not complete his work before the *Beagle* needed major repairs and her crew needed to be rested. He was also

Tsunami

The great wave that swept onto the coast of Chile after the earthquake felt by Charles Darwin is called a tsunami. It happens if an earthquake suddenly raises the seabed. The rising seabed lifts the sea above it. Then the bulge of water flows away in all directions. When it reaches the shallow water near land, it rears up into a giant wave. A tsunami is far more powerful and damaging than any normal wave on the seashore.

worried by the need to overload the ship with supplies. She was supposed to carry up to eight months' stores, but twice we set sail weighed down dangerously by ten months' provisions. A second ship could share the load and carry out some of the survey work. To this end, Captain FitzRoy bought a small American schooner called *Unicorn* and had it refitted as a survey ship. He renamed it *Adventure*. It seemed a sensible way forward."

He said that FitzRoy had told his officers, "She is a fine vessel of 170 tonnes and an excellent sea-boat. If the Admiralty agrees to the provisioning and payment of men, this day will be an important one in the history of the *Beagle*. Perhaps it may shorten our voyage. Anyhow, it is always more pleasant to sail in company than alone. The *Adventure* will break the boredom of an empty ocean."

Wickham continued, "The captain expected the Admiralty in London to support him and repay him for the cost of buying and refitting the *Adventure*."

FitzRoy had said, "I believe that their Lordships will approve of what I have done, but if I am wrong, there will be no cost to the government, because I am responsible for the cost of the vessel, and am able to pay it."

"Alas," said Wickham, "when the Admiralty learned what the captain had done, they did not approve. Not only did they refuse to pay the cost, but they also told off the captain for his action and demanded that he sell the *Adventure*. As ordered, he sold the *Adventure* and paid off her crew, but he was so upset that he decided to give up his command of the *Beagle*. We were worried for his state of mind. By good luck, we persuaded him to change his mind and continue with the voyage."

I had said as a joke that my job was to keep the captain sane, but I was very worried that this near-disaster had happened while I was away from the ship for several months. Perhaps it was not a joke after all.

Chapter summary:

- Darwin sets sail with the *Beagle* in 1891. It is captained by Robert FitzRoy.
- He collects many animal specimens from the oceans and islands they visit during the *Beagle*'s voyage.
- In the Andes mountains, Darwin realises that slow but powerful forces beneath the Earth's surface have shaped the land over millions of years.
- Darwin and the crew witness a terrible earthquake in the Bay of Concepcion in Chile.
- FitzRoy threatens to quit as captain of the *Beagle* over a disagreement with the Admiralty. The crew persuade him to stay on.

Chapter 3
1835

On 7th September, 1835, the *Beagle* left the coast of South America and sailed west into the open ocean. Eight days and 600 miles later we spotted land. It was Chatham Island, the most eastern of the Galapagos Islands. We were to spend a month amongst these islands while the crew on the *Beagle* mapped their coasts and the surrounding waters. Although these islands were tiny in size, their importance would later prove to be enormous.

These strange little worlds lie on the equator. They are mounds of black volcanic rock, the tops of volcanoes that grew with each eruption until they appeared above the ocean. They were mostly covered with leafless brushwood and small trees. The *Beagle* put a party of us ashore to explore. The sun-baked rock was as hot as a stove. I pushed a thermometer into the black volcanic sand and it went off the scale at 58 degrees centigrade.

It's a wonder that anything could survive there, but these islands crawled with numerous crabs and ugly lizards called iguanas. There were flocks of small birds. Giant tortoises were abundant too. The tortoises were so big and heavy that I could scarcely lift one. The *Beagle*'s crew seized 18 of them and took them to the ship for fresh meat. The scorched land, hard as black iron, and its strange creatures looked like a vision of another planet.

I collected large numbers of reptiles and birds. They and all the other plants and creatures must

The Galapagos Islands

The Galapagos Island are a group of 21 volcanic islands and more than 100 rocks and islets in the Pacific Ocean about 900 kilometres (600 miles) west of Ecuador. They formed about five million years ago above a 'hot spot' where the Earth's crust is being heated and melted from below, producing volcanoes. The lava that erupted from the volcanoes cooled down and grew in size until it emerged from the ocean to form the islands. The names of the islands have changed since Darwin's time. Darwin's Chatham Island is now called San Cristobal and Albemarle Island is now called Isabela.

have arrived from other parts of the world after the islands formed. Some of the birds looked like species I had seen in South America.

On Albemarle Island I discovered lizards up to four feet in length that looked like the iguanas living on the seashore, but the inland lizards were coloured orange-yellow and red, and they lived in burrows. The coastal iguanas fed on seaweed, while their inland cousins ate berries and leaves. We collected 40 of them with ease, mainly for food.

One strange thing about the islands was that there were no insect swarms like there were everywhere else in the tropics. Because of this, most of the birds ate seeds. Their beaks were the right size and shape for cracking hard seeds instead of feeding on soft insects. The birds included mockingbirds, doves and finches. The mockingbirds looked like birds I had seen in Chile. I collected birds from three of the islands. The different species were quite alike in size and colour. They flocked together and behaved in the same way. It was even difficult to tell the males from the females. They were very confusing little creatures. I made things worse by not labelling which islands the birds I collected came from. I would later regret this.

On Charles Island, we found a group of about 200 prisoners who had been transported from Ecuador. They led a very risky 'Robinson Crusoe' life. The acting governor, Mr Lawson, was an Englishman. He told us that the main source of food on the islands was tortoise-meat and he said of the creatures, "The numbers of these great beasts have been much reduced in recent years. Once, a visiting ship's crew might easily drag 200 to the shore, but now only a fraction of that number could be caught. I fear the remaining tortoises might last for only another 20 years."

The prisoners told us that each island had its own type of tortoise and that the creatures

Robinson Crusoe

Robinson Crusoe is a novel written by Daniel Defoe and published in 1719. It tells the story of a man, Robinson Crusoe, who runs away from home to travel the world as a sailor. During his travels, he is shipwrecked on a desert island. He lives off the land and survives for 27 years until he is rescued by a passing ship.

differed in the shape of their shells. Mr Lawson went further. He said, "I can easily tell which island any tortoise has come from." I doubted this, because the tortoises I saw on two of the islands were so similar that it was hard to tell one from another. Later, I was to discover that I was wrong. I did not collect any of the tortoises, even though many empty shells were lying around and might have been taken to the ship easily. I thought these creatures must have been brought to the islands from elsewhere by the crews of visiting ships for food.

After a month surveying the many islands of the group, the *Beagle* set sail for Polynesia. I helped the crew to eat the tortoises taken from the islands and then I watched as the shells were thrown overboard. It did not occur to me to save them for my collection. I thought the islands to be too recently risen from the sea for their plants and animals to be of any interest or importance.

MY GOODNESS, WHAT AN UGLY REPTILE!
YOU COULD FRY AN EGG ON THE ROCK!
HIIIISSSSSSS!
I'D HISS TOO IF I HAD TO EAT PRICKLY CACTUS.

IT CAN CARRY ME EASILY.
THE BIRDS HAVE NO FEAR OF PEOPLE.
THEY ALL LOOK THE SAME TO ME!

How wrong I was.

With more than 3,000 miles to go until we reached land, I had time to think again about my Galapagos specimens. When I looked at them more closely I began to see differences between the birds, so perhaps the stories I'd heard about the birds and tortoises being different on each island were true after all. I started to wonder what this might mean.

The *Beagle* continued its epic voyage around the globe, calling at Tahiti, New Zealand and Australia. We stopped at the Keeling Islands midway between Australia and Ceylon to investigate coral atolls. There were two different theories to explain how they formed. They might form on the seabed and grow up to the surface or they might form at the surface. But which was correct? If corals formed at great depth, we could expect to find evidence of coral deep below the surface. However, we found no living coral below 20 fathoms (36 metres), so they must form higher up in the water, near the surface.

We sailed on to Mauritius, the Cape of Good Hope at the southern tip of Africa, St Helena and Ascension. As we set sail from Ascension, anxious to return to England, we thought we were on our last leg of the home journey. However, to our great surprise and disappointment we made our second crossing of the Atlantic Ocean to Brazil. The reason was that Captain FitzRoy wanted to check that the maps he had made were accurate. Then finally we set sail for home.

Coral atolls

A coral atoll is a ring-shaped coral reef with water (a lagoon) in the middle. To form, it needs a volcano. An underwater volcano erupts again and again until its top appears above the water, forming a new island. Coral grows in the shallow water on the volcano's sides. Over millions of years, the volcano sinks back into the sea. As it sinks, the coral grows upwards towards the light. Waves pile up sand, rocks and broken coral on the reef, forming the ring-shaped atoll.

Chapter summary:

- Darwin and the crew of the *Beagle* visit the Galapagos islands and collect new species of reptiles and birds.
- Darwin notices that there are differences between the tortoises and birds found on different islands. He starts to wonder what could be the causes of this.

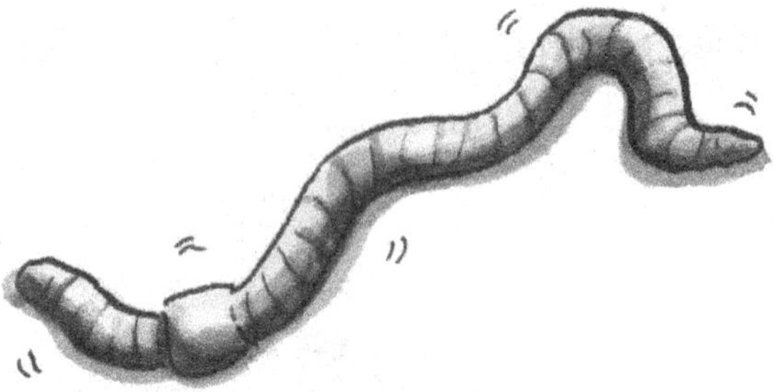

Chapter 4

1836

The *Beagle* docked at Falmouth on the south coast of England on 2 October, 1836. Our 'two-year expedition' had in fact kept us from our homes for five years. From Falmouth, the journey home to Shrewsbury took two days by stagecoach at the gallop. The woods and fields looked more beautiful to me than I could ever remember. My fellow travellers looked a little surprised when I gazed out at the countryside and said, "The wide world does not contain so happy a view as the rich cultivated land of England."

I arrived home so late that everyone in the house had already gone to bed. I went to my room and, exhausted, fell into a deep sleep. My father and sisters had such a surprise when I entered the breakfast room in the morning. My sister Susan looked me up and down and exclaimed, "You are thin, brother. We shall have to feed you up."

My first thought was to have my last collection of specimens taken off the *Beagle* and sent to specialists for study. I gave some of the plants to Henslow, the man I had to thank for offering me his place on the expedition. And I gave mammal specimens to the Zoological Society.

Then I turned my attention to where I was to live. At first, I stayed in Cambridge, but I soon realised that I needed to be where the experts are, in London, so I moved to the capital. It was quite a contrast to Cambridge. London was a busy city of two million people, lit up at night by gas lamps.

As I explored London, I discovered that I

had become famous. My travels and works had become widely known. I worked during the day, writing science reports, papers and lectures, and went to dinners where I made useful contacts in the evenings. The Geological Society applauded my talk about the west coast of South America having been pushed upwards by earthquakes. I was so pleased with their response that I was like a peacock admiring his tail.

Meanwhile, I was more certain that one species could change into another, a process called transmutation. I wasn't the only naturalist to have these thoughts, but so far no one knew why or how it might happen. What was the driving force that changed species from one to another? This had to be the focus of my work. But any public mention of transmutation was fiercely opposed by those who believed that all species are created by God and then forever remain unchanged, so I kept my thoughts to myself.

I was troubled by not being able to make sense of the birds I had collected on the Galapagos Islands. I gave them to John Gould, a bird expert at the Zoological Society and said to him, "I am at a loss to know what to make of these little creatures. They appear to me to be different kinds of blackbirds, finches, gross-beaks and wrens. I think they are of little importance, but make of them what you will. If anyone can untangle their mystery, you can."

A few days later, I returned to the society to hear what Gould thought. I was astonished when he said, "All the birds are ground finches which are so odd that they form an entirely new group of twelve species."

Instantly, I realised their great importance to my work and I regretted not labelling them with which islands they had come from. Others on the *Beagle*, including Captain FitzRoy, had also collected birds on the islands and luckily they had

Evolution before Darwin

The first person to develop a scientific theory of evolution was a French naturalist called Jean-Baptiste Lamarck (1744–1829). He thought living creatures continually came into existence from non-living matter and evolved into more and more complex creatures. He thought that creatures changed their behaviour to suit their environment and that these changes in behaviour physically changed the creatures. He also thought that these physical changes that happened in a single lifetime were passed on from one generation to another.

labelled their specimens more fully. When I looked at them, I found that each species belonged to one island. It was the same for the mockingbirds – each species to an island. It suggested that after the birds arrived on the islands from the mainland they had changed so much that they had become new species, and they had changed differently on each island. The Galapagos tortoises appeared to have changed in the same way. But what was it that changed them? And did the changes happen gradually over many generations or did they happen suddenly in one blow?

I tried to discuss the matter with Richard Owen, an outstanding naturalist, without revealing my private thoughts. Owen quickly made his feelings clear. He thundered, "No creature can reach beyond the limits of its own species. How could it occur? And any talk of humans evolving from apes is an abomination." His views, that all creatures – including apes

The first zoo

The Zoological Society of London was formed in 1826 for the study of animals. Two years later, its Zoological Gardens opened to the society's members. The gardens housed a collection of animals from all over the world. In 1847, the gardens were opened to the public, who quickly started calling it 'the zoo'. London Zoo, as it became known, was the world's first zoo.

and humans – were made exactly as they are by God, were widely held.

Then I thought of the fossil bones I had collected. They were the bones of creatures that existed in the distant past, but they do not exist now. I wondered if the giant llamas and sloths of the past could have changed, or evolved, to become the smaller llamas and sloths that live today. But some fossils belonged to creatures that have no living relatives today. They had died out altogether. But how is that possible if species can evolve? If the climate had changed, for example, why could the animals not have changed to suit their new conditions? Perhaps, I thought, species have a certain lifespan in the same way that individual creatures have a lifespan, after which they die out.

There was another problem. The Galapagos finches suggested that creatures had to live separately from each other on different islands to evolve into different species. However, creatures on the mainland had evolved into different species too, yet they were free to roam and mix with each other. It was all a great puzzle. I wanted to give all my time to solving it, but I couldn't. I was rushing to finish rewriting my journal of the

Fossils

Fossils are the remains of plants and animals that lived a very long time ago, perhaps millions or even billions of years ago. Most creatures that died were quickly eaten, but some were buried under earth or mud before this happened. Their soft, fleshy parts rotted away, leaving the bones. Water in the ground seeped into the bones. Then minerals in the water slowly replaced the bone, forming a fossil.

Beagle voyage so that it could be published, while also working on a multi-volume work, *Zoology of the Voyage of HMS Beagle*. The cost of producing this book was so great that Henslow helped me to get money from the government so that it could be done.

It was at this time that my health began to worsen, probably because of the fast pace of my work. In September 1837, I saw my doctor and told him, "Of late, anything that worries me completely knocks me off keel and brings on a violent palpitation of the heart."

When he finished his examination, he said, "I strongly advise you to stop all work immediately and leave for the country to rest."

I took his advice and went to stay at Maer Hall, the Staffordshire home of my uncle, Josiah Wedgwood. But I had little chance of rest, because my cousin Emma wore me out with her questions about my travels. Not only that. While Uncle Josiah walked with me in the grounds, he showed me a patch of earth and said, "Cinders were spread here a year ago, but now there is no sign of them. It is my belief that earthworms have taken them underground."

He thought it was a matter of no importance,

but it greatly interested me and set me off on years of research with these humble creatures – as if I needed more work!

On my return to London, I met with breeders of dogs, cats, fancy pigeons and cattle. It had occurred to me that they did the same thing deliberately that nature did by chance. They bred animals to bring out particular qualities and traits. They changed species to improve them. They did it by choosing which animals were allowed to mate and produce young. They called it selective breeding. For instance, if they wanted to breed dogs with a particular quality, like long ears, they would breed two dogs with long ears so that their puppies would have them too. But what was the process that did this in nature, where all creatures have the possibility of producing young? It was a baffling problem.

I was becoming more convinced that humans must be subject to the same natural processes as other creatures. If I was right, it follows that humans must have evolved from more primitive apes. And so we very likely share some qualities with existing apes. I saw this for myself at the Zoological Society's gardens in London. There, I saw an orangutan called Jenny. I told my sister Susan, "The keeper showed Jenny an apple, but he would not give it to her. The ape threw herself on her back, kicking and crying like a naughty child. When she stopped whining she was given the apple. She took it and sat in a chair eating it with the most contented expression on her face." Jenny's human-like behaviour led me to believe that my ideas about human evolution were correct.

Then I read a book that finally made everything clear to me. It was called *Essay on the Principle of Population* by Thomas Malthus. Malthus said that if the number of people on Earth continued to grow, after a time there would not be enough food for them all, and so population growth would stop. He worked out that the number of people on Earth could double every 25 years, but it didn't. The growth in population was much slower than this. It was slowed by disease, war, famine and other setbacks. I suddenly realised that the same struggles take place everywhere in nature. Animals compete with each other for food and for mates. They suffer from diseases and are killed by droughts, floods, fires and predators. And each of these many daily battles could be a driving force for evolution.

Individual animals are not identical to each other. They vary a little from one creature to another. Normally, these small variations come and go from one generation to another and serve no purpose. But if a group of animals faces difficulties, perhaps because of disease or changes in the climate, these natural variations may give some animals a small advantage over the others. Animals that are by chance a little faster or bigger

Jenny the orangutan

Jenny was the first orangutan to be put on display at London Zoo. She was bought by the zoo from a private owner in 1837 and kept in the zoo's heated giraffe house. She died two years later and was replaced by another orangutan, which was also named Jenny. In 1842, Queen Victoria saw the second Jenny and found her human-like appearance disagreeable.

or stronger, or more resistant to disease, are more likely to survive and pass on their improved characteristics to the next generation. Creatures without these improved characteristics are less likely to survive long enough to produce healthy young. For example, the fastest antelope is more likely to escape a predator and live for long enough to pass on its speed to its children. Slower antelopes are more likely to be eaten before they can have children. So, over time, antelopes become faster. Species that can't adapt to their changing environment might die out altogether. This is surely how natural selection works, gradually changing one species into another species. This was my 'Eureka Moment'. I had it. I finally had my theory of evolution by natural selection.

At the end of 1838 another, umm, 'difficulty' started to fill my thoughts. I told a friend, "I am 29 years old, my heart is troubling me and I am alone. We poor bachelors are only half men, creeping like caterpillars through the world, alone. My life is empty, measured only by the chapters and pages of my books and scientific papers. As for a wife, that most interesting specimen of animals, who knows whether I shall ever capture one."

My friend told me, "Well, Charles, you must do something about it. You're a clever man, so you must surely be able to find a solution."

Marriage is a serious business and it needs a lot of thought. I applied the mind of a scientist to the matter. I drew a line down the middle of a sheet of paper and wrote the heading 'Marry' on one side and 'Not Marry' on the other side. Then I listed the advantages and disadvantages of each course of action. If I were not to marry, I could travel wherever I wished whenever I wished, and work whatever hours I wished. But I would be alone with no one to keep me company in my old age. If I were to marry, I would have a close, lifelong friendship with someone and perhaps children. But it would also mean losing my freedom and having to work for money. Perhaps I could be a Cambridge professor of geology – or zoology? On balance, I thought marriage would not be so bad. Other men seem to survive it. Why not me? So, marriage it was to be.

The next question was – who should I marry? Who would have me? I made a list of all the suitable women in my circle of friends. I quickly thought of my cousin Emma. I saw no reason to delay, so I travelled to her home, Maer House, and proposed marriage to her. She accepted. But it wasn't long before she raised a most awkward matter. She said, "I fear that our opinions on the most important subject might differ widely." Of course, she was talking about religion. It would indeed divide us.

GENTLEMEN, MY TALK TONIGHT CONCERNS THE GEOLOGY OF SOUTH AMERICA.

THE ROYAL SOCIETY'S ROYAL MEDAL FOR 1853 IS AWARDED TO CHARLES DARWIN.
THERE ARE IMPORTANT CONTACTS TO BE MADE HERE.

YOU CREATED THIS BREED OF HEN?
YES, I DID. I CAN PRODUCE ANY FORM OF BIRD YOU WISH WITHIN SIX YEARS BY SELECTIVE BREEDING.

THIS EXCELLENT BOOK BY THOMAS MALTHUS HAS GIVEN ME THE FINAL PIECE OF MY THEORY.
COULD THIS BE HOW SPECIES EVOLVE?
YES, I THINK THIS IS HOW IT IS, THE TREE OF EVOLUTION.
I think...

We were married at St Peter's Church, Maer, on 29 January, 1839. After so much time alone, I now shared my life with Emma – and of course our new domestic staff. Our first-born, William Erasmus, arrived before the end of the year. It was a joyous time, but I was still often unwell, which made it difficult to work. Emma nursed me while she was expecting our second child, Anne Elizabeth. I often suffered from shivering, headaches and sickness. I thought it must be due to the great stress of keeping my true thoughts on evolution secret from my friends and family, who would surely disapprove of them. Most people believed that God had made the world just as it is. I was scared of what people would think of me if my secret was ever to be discovered.

London no longer provided the comfort and quiet that I longed for. I wanted to be rid of its dirt and noise. And so, we found this lovely village of Down, and in it Down House. We moved here in

September 1842. It was the perfect, quiet country home that we'd hoped for, especially as Emma was expecting another baby. I spent month after month working on my theory of evolution in secret, filling book after book with my notes, but I knew it would be impossible to publish it. It would have been seen as a betrayal of my friends and my wife because of their religious beliefs. I was in constant turmoil over it. Then I hit on a solution. I thought it likely that I might die in the near future because of my poor health, so I decided to leave my writings on evolution to Emma with instructions to have them published after my death.

Meanwhile, I busied myself writing books and essays on 'safer' subjects such as geology, barnacles and fossils. Our family suffered a terrible blow at this time with the death of our dear daughter Annie. She was taken from us by scarlet fever.

By the mid-1850s, a few more scientists were

beginning to talk openly about evolution, but they couldn't explain how it might happen. Finally, I could keep my secret no longer. I told a close friend, Charles Lyell, my theory of evolution by natural selection. He listened patiently and thought about what I had told him for some time before he said, "I cannot bring myself to agree with you because of my religious beliefs, but I strongly urge you to publish your theory without delay or I fear you may be beaten to it by someone else. If that were to happen, then all your work will have been for nothing."

At first, I planned to publish a short paper, but I quickly realised that I had so much information to fit in that a large book would be needed. I threw myself into the work. Then everything changed with the arrival of the postman one day. The date is burned into my memory – 15 June, 1858. When I read the contents of the letter, I went straight to Lyell and cried at him, "Your words have come true. I am beaten."

Another naturalist had produced his own theory of evolution by natural selection. I felt that I had lost everything. What was I to do?

Scarlet fever

Scarlet fever is an infectious disease caused by bacteria. It mainly affects children, causing a rash, fever and sore throat. Without treatment, it spreads throughout the body and eventually affects vital organs including the heart, lungs and kidneys. Today, it is treated by antibiotics, but in Darwin's time there was no effective treatment, so children who caught scarlet fever often died.

Chapter summary:

- Darwin returns to England in 1836.
- Darwin starts to believe in the idea of transmutation: that one animal species can turn into another over time. He begins to think that all species, including humans, have evolved over time from earlier species.
- Reading Thomas Malthus' work convinces Darwin that the struggle for survival drives evolution. The traits inherited from their parents will give some animals an advantage in their environment which means that they're able to have offspring and keep passing on those same characteristics.
- Darwin begins to suffer from poor health. He marries his cousin Emma in 1839 and starts a family. The Darwins move to Down House in the countryside.

Chapter 5

1858

I'd received a letter from a naturalist called Alfred Russel Wallace. While he was collecting specimens in the Malay Archipelago, he started thinking about how the various species came to be as they are. He put his ideas down in a twenty-page article and, because he knew I had some interest in the matter, he sent it to me. When I looked at it, I couldn't believe what I was reading. His article talked about variations in species being pushed further and further from the parent species by the struggle for existence. I told Lyell, "I never saw a more striking coincidence. If Wallace had seen my essay on this same subject written 16 years ago in 1842, he could not have written a better summary of it."

I feared that whatever I did after this, whatever I published, it might now look as if I had stolen my ideas from Wallace. It was a disaster. Lyell wondered what to do and came up with a novel solution. He said, "I think the two theories, yours and Wallace's, should be announced jointly."

I didn't have to think about it for very long. I readily agreed with him, but I thought it could still look to others as if I was stealing Wallace's work. I couldn't think what else I might do. I left it all to my close friends, Charles Lyell and Joseph Hooker, to arrange, because I had something infinitely more important to deal with. Scarlet fever was once again sweeping through our village. Three children had already died and now the worst nightmare came to pass. The fever took our dear little baby Charles from us. He was barely 18 months old. When Hooker tried to discuss Wallace's article with me I told him, "I cannot think now. I hardly care about it. I will do whatever you suggest."

Wallace, still in the Far East, was contacted and informed of the plan. He agreed. I wrote to him and assured him that "I had nothing to do with leading Lyell and Hooker to their decision."

Our two theories were presented at the Linnean Society in London on the evening of 1 July, 1858. The society's secretary read Wallace's article and my own to an audience of about 30 fellows. I did not go. I was still laid low with grief and illness. I heard later that the articles were listened to in respectful silence, and there was little reaction or interest in them. No one thought them to be of much importance. I received the news with relief. At least no one was calling for me to be strung up from the nearest tree for going against what millions of Christians believed!

When I was well enough I continued my work on *Natural Selection*. I sent each chapter to Hooker as I finished it for his comments. Once

The Linnean Society

The Linnean Society was formed in London in 1788 for the study of natural history and evolution, making it the world's oldest surviving natural history society. It was named after the Swedish scientist, Carl von Linne (1707–1778), also known by the Latin form of his name, Carolus Linnaeus. He invented the method that is still used today by scientists for naming species.

I nearly lost a chapter when it got mixed up with scrap paper at Hooker's house. His children scribbled and drew on a quarter of the pages before Hooker noticed. Luckily, he managed to save them all.

The manuscript grew longer and longer. I thought it might never end. To cut it down I removed dozens of illustrations, hundreds of references and lots of text. In doing so, I got it down to 155,000 words. I was pleasantly surprised when I received the manuscript back from Hooker with his notes. I told him, "You do not seem to have found many mistakes. It was nearly all written from memory, so I was particularly fearful."

Lyell found a publisher, John Murray, for my book. Murray had already published my *Beagle* Journal, but I was worried that he might reject *Natural Selection*. He'd refused other books that he thought would upset Christians. I asked Lyell, "Does he know anything about the book? Perhaps you could tell him that it doesn't discuss the origin of man."

Lyell spoke to him and told Darwin that he thought it would be alright. Murray seemed more interested in finding the right title for the book. I told him, "I thought of calling it *An Abstract of an Essay on the Origin of Species and Varieties through Natural Selection.*"

As soon as he heard it, his face fell. He said, "Mr Darwin, I fancy your title will rob us of our profits. I suggest we shorten it to *On the Origin of Species and Varieties by Natural Selection.*"

I thought on it further and changed it to *On the Origin of Species by Means of Natural Selection*. Still, Murray didn't appear to see much promise in the book. At first, he said he would print only 500 copies, but he increased this to 1,250 copies. We planned to publish the book in November 1859. Now, the race was on to check the pages and make last minute corrections before the book was due to be printed.

When I read the corrected pages, I was very disappointed with the poor quality of my writing. I made lots of changes to the text.

Under all the pressure and stress my health began to fail again, but I had no choice but to continue. I was driven by a strong wish to finish the book and finally rid my mind of the whole subject. By the end, I could barely manage 20 minutes of work at my desk without terrible stomach pain and vomiting.

The corrected pages were sent to Lyell for his comments. I was worried about what he might say, but he seemed pleased with my work. I finished my work on the book at the end of October and immediately fled to Wells House at Ilkley by the Yorkshire Moors to take the water cure. When Joseph Hooker asked about my health, I told him, "I am in a dreadful state. One of my legs has swelled up like elephantiasis. My eyes are almost closed and I am covered with rashes and fiery boils. I am in Hell."

My mood improved at the beginning of November when a package arrived for me. It was the first copy of my book. Printed on cream paper and bound in a green cover, I thought it was a thing of beauty. After so many years of work, trouble, stress and worry, I couldn't quite believe that it was finally here, resting in my hands. But my pride didn't last long. Mr Murray asked me to write notes to be sent out with the first free copies of the book. I suddenly realised that the book was soon going to be read by people who were certain to be offended and angered by it. I wrote a card to my old teacher Henslow that said, "I fear you will not approve of your pupil." And I wrote to Wallace, "God knows what the public will think of it."

I dreaded what they would say after they'd read the book. All I could do was wait for the storm that was surely to come.

The water cure

The water cure is the use of water to treat illnesses, relieve pain and generally improve health.

The water is usually mineral water from natural springs. Using water for health reasons is also called hydrotherapy. It was very popular in the eighteenth and nineteenth centuries. People who took the water cure 'enjoyed' hot and cold showers and baths, being wrapped in wet towels, drinking lots of natural spring water, exercise and a strict diet.

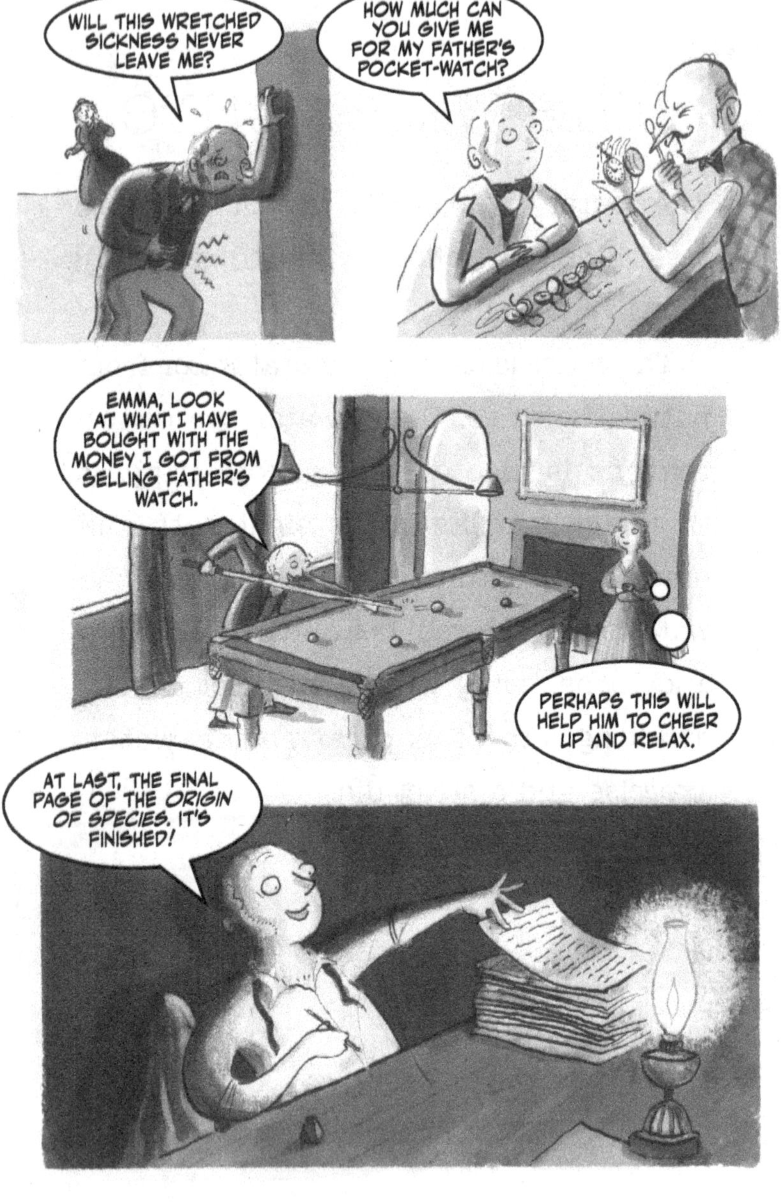
WILL THIS WRETCHED SICKNESS NEVER LEAVE ME?
HOW MUCH CAN YOU GIVE ME FOR MY FATHER'S POCKET-WATCH?
EMMA, LOOK AT WHAT I HAVE BOUGHT WITH THE MONEY I GOT FROM SELLING FATHER'S WATCH.
PERHAPS THIS WILL HELP HIM TO CHEER UP AND RELAX.
AT LAST, THE FINAL PAGE OF THE *ORIGIN OF SPECIES*. IT'S FINISHED!

THE COLD WATER IS VERY REFRESHING.
MR DARWIN, A PACKAGE HAS ARRIVED FOR YOU.
I CAN'T BELIEVE IT. FINALLY, MY *ORIGIN OF SPECIES* IS HERE.
ORIGIN
SPECIES
DARWIN

Chapter summary:

- Darwin worries that his ideas will be overshadowed by the similar ones put forward by the naturalist Alfred Wallace. Darwin's friends see to it that both naturalists' work are presented at the same time at the Linnean Society on 1 July, 1858. The audience is uninterested.
- Darwin struggles through poor health to complete his book: *On the Origin of Species by Means of Natural Selection*. He is worried that the book will anger and offend Christians.

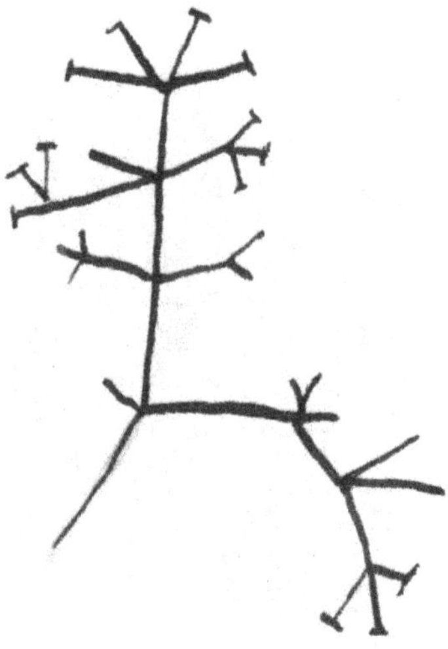

Chapter 6

1859

The Origin of Species was published on 24 November, 1859, while I was still recovering at Wells House. The first news I received about it was good. Booksellers had placed orders for 1,500 copies, 250 more than John Murray planned to print, so work began on a second edition. The first letters I received from readers were surprisingly good too. One from a vicar said, "If you be right, I must give up much that I have believed." And he really meant it. He thought it wonderful that

God had created creatures that could evolve and change in the way I described. I couldn't have been happier. It was better than I ever hoped for.

Then the reviews printed in newspapers and journals arrived and they were harsher. They condemned the book. They believed that all species were created by God. To them, the idea that nature could change species by itself was laughable. My younger friends were kinder. They were more open-minded, but they had concerns about what my theory meant for man. They disliked the idea that man could have evolved from apes.

Adam Sedgwick, who had taught me geology, wrote to me, "I have read your book with more pain than pleasure. Parts of it I admired greatly; parts I laughed at till my sides were sore; other parts I read with sorrow; because I think them utterly false." Henslow, my great friend and mentor, thought the book was a marvellous collection of facts, but said I had pushed my theory too far. The best he could say was that, "it is a stumble in the right direction." A stumble!

I was told later that my name had been put forward by the Prime Minister for a knighthood. But once the *Origin of Species* was published, the queen was advised that an honour for its author would look like royal approval for the theory of evolution by natural selection. As the head of the Church of England, she could not be seen to support such a godless theory, so the Prime Minister's request was rejected.

I thought my book would be of interest only to educated people, so I was surprised to hear of travellers and passers-by buying copies at a bookstall outside Waterloo Station. Mr Murray told me he was going to print another 3,000 copies to meet the demand.

My book was used in discussions about a new museum of natural history. Richard Owen, the head of natural history collections at the British Museum, told Parliament, "Visitors to the British Museum want to see all the different creatures so that they might judge for themselves what evidence there is for Mr Darwin's theory of evolution by natural selection. But I am ashamed to tell them that I cannot show them any of those creatures, because we do not have the space for them. Surely, there ought to be space somewhere, and, if not in the British Museum, where is it to be found?" He got his way and Parliament decided that a Natural History Museum was to be built.

Cartoonists and illustrators were quick to have their fun with the book and its writer. I often came across sketches of myself with the body of an ape in books and newspapers. My book and theory were discussed at many an angry meeting. I did not attend these gatherings because of my poor health. At one debate in Oxford, a gentleman stood up and said, I have read the *Origin of Species*

The Natural History Museum

The Natural History Museum opened in London in 1881, the year before Darwin's death. It was headed by Richard Owen, the man who had campaigned for it. A statue of Owen sat in the museum's main hall until 2009, when it was replaced by a life-size statue of Darwin. The museum is visited by more than four million people every year.

with the most awful pain.' Then he held up a large Bible high above his head and said, "I ask all of you here today to believe in God, not man." He was none other than Robert FitzRoy, the captain of the *Beagle*

I had always thought of the *Origin of Species* as an introduction to my theory of evolution by natural selection. Now, it was time to start work on 'the big book', the book that would give the whole story. And this time it would have to deal with the trickiest subject – the descent of man from earlier creatures. As usual, I took on far too much work. At the same time as writing the big book, I wrote books and scientific papers about orchids, insect-eating plants, vegetable fertilisation, different forms of flowers, the power of movement in plants and the Malay Archipelago.

The big book, now called *The Descent of Man, and Selection in Relation to Sex*, was finally published in 1871. John Murray published it as two 450-page volumes. It was so successful that the books sold out after only three weeks. John Murray had to have more printed. By the time it was published, most scientists and many others accepted evolution as a fact, so *Descent* did not cause the same outrage as the *Origin of Species*. I told my old friend, Joseph Hooker, "Everybody is talking about it without being shocked."

THIS DARWIN CHAP HAS SURELY LOST HIS MIND!
THIS BOOK THAT PRESUMES TO EXPLAIN THE ORIGIN OF SPECIES IS AN ABOMINATION. IT IS THE WORK OF THE DEVIL!
THE PRIME MINISTER REQUESTS A KNIGHTHOOD FOR MISTER CHARLES DARWIN.
I THINK NOT MA'AM. THE CHURCH RESPECTFULLY ADVISES AGAINST IT.

WAS YOUR GRANNY A MONKEY, MISTER DARWIN?
THEY'RE LAUGHING AT ME.
LET THEM HAVE THEIR FUN. THEY WILL SOON TIRE OF IT.
WHEN THIS SHOP SOLD MY *ORIGIN OF SPECIES*, A MOB SMASHED THE WINDOW.
THEY'VE COME ROUND TO YOUR WAY OF THINKING, CHARLES.

Chapter summary:

- Darwin's book, *On the Origin of Species*, is condemned by the press, the Church of England and many scientists when it is published in 1859. Darwin is mocked and criticised for his revolutionary ideas.
- However, the book is a big success. Darwin's next book, *The Descent of Man*, also sells out when it is published in 1871. By this time, Darwin's ideas have become widely accepted.

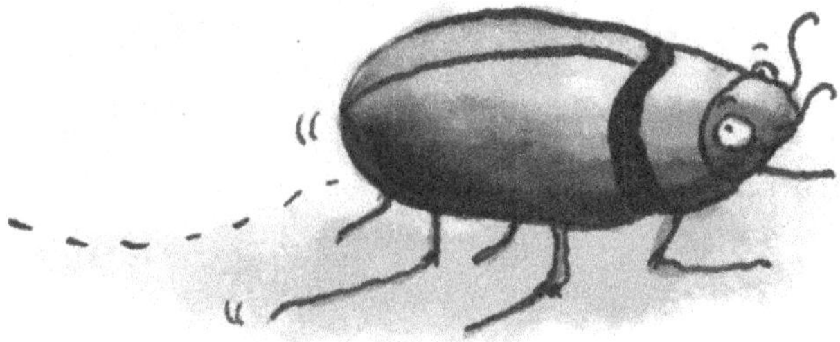

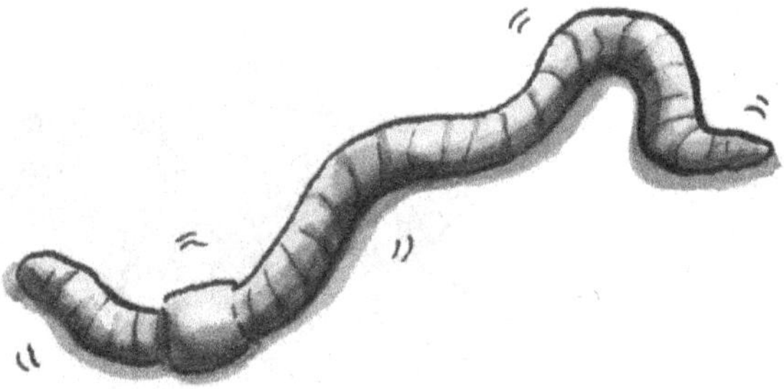

Epilogue

1876

Darwin spent a few moments in silent thought, contemplating his extraordinary life. He looked back on his childhood, remembering the days he had spent watching birds, exploring the countryside and collecting curious critters to examine. That little boy had come a very long way indeed, traversing the globe and publishing his research.

Smiling fondly, he thought of how many people

had helped him along the way. He remembered his father who, though initially reluctant, had agreed to support and even fund his adventures on the *Beagle*. And he thought of Uncle Josiah, the man who had changed his father's mind and convinced him to take his place on that fateful expedition.

What would have happened if he never went on that trip? Darwin shuddered at the thought. His life could have been so different. Was he always destined to be a man of science, or would he have become a clergyman to please his family? Perhaps Alfred Russel Wallace would have penned the *Origin of Species* instead. Without his research driving him forwards, Darwin could not imagine how differently his life may have played out.

Snapping out of his thoughts, he turned to his own son, Francis, who had been listening to his story. Darwin said "It's all been quite an adventure – which brings us to our new project.

Now to set it all down on paper."

On 28 May, 1876, Darwin took out a fresh sheet of paper and wrote across the top, *Recollections of the Development of my Mind and Character*. He finished the book in less than three months. Although Darwin didn't intend to publish it, it was edited by Francis and published along with some of his letters five years after his death as *The life and letters of Charles Darwin, including an autobiographical chapter*. Francis clearly inherited his father's liking for long book titles!

Darwin's last book, *The Formation of Vegetable Mould through the Action of Worms, with Observations of their Habits*, was published just six months before he died. It described 40 years of observations and research with earthworms. It quickly outsold the *Origin of Species*, selling 6,000 copies in its first year alone.

On the evening of 18 April, 1882, Darwin suffered a heart attack at Down House. Perhaps sensing that the end was near, he turned and said to his wife, "Tell all my children to remember how good they have always been to me." After a short while he added, "I am not the least afraid to die." Darwin eventually died in his home on the following day, at 4.00 p.m. 19 April, 1882.

He had expected to be buried at St Mary's churchyard near Down House. However, his fellow scientists thought that a grander resting place would be much more fitting. A campaign to bury him beside other great scientists in Westminster Abbey quickly gained momentum. To be buried in Westminster Abbey was considered a great honour and a sign of a person's importance. When the plan was put to his family they agreed. However, some local people were unhappy that he was not to be buried in the village, the place he had spent most of his life.

For more than 40 years, Darwin had suffered from his deteriorating health. He had developed stomach pain, vomiting, eczema, boils, headaches, fever, fainting and heart problems, especially at times of great stress. In the 1860s, he grew his bushy beard in an attempt to hide his skin problems and avoid the daily pain of shaving. The cause of his illness baffled doctors during his lifetime. They could not agree on a unanimous diagnosis, which made treatment extremely difficult. Since then, doctors have suggested a number of possible causes.

One prominent theory suggests that Darwin was suffering from a condition called Chagas disease. This is a tropical disease spread by blood-sucking insects called kissing bugs. Found in South America, these creatures are known to bite a victim's lips or face, thus earning them the name 'kissing bugs'. Evidence for this theory points towards Darwin's *Beagle* diary entry for 26 March, 1835, whilst he was explored Mendoza Province of Argentina. Here, Darwin recalled an attack by a blood-sucking insect, known locally as a Benchuca. Darwin described this animal as a great wingless black bug, measuring about an inch long. Experimenting with one of these creatures, Darwin found that it became swollen with blood after ten minutes sucking, and did not need another blood-meal for two weeks. The bug he described sounded very much like a kissing bug, which could provide an answer to his mysterious ailment.

By the time of his death, Darwin's theory of evolution by natural selection had already gained general acceptance in Britain. Since then, living species have produced more evidence to support his thinking. Though Darwin's evolutionary theory has adjusted over the years, it remains a touchstone for modern biologists, continually driving new discoveries. His revolutionary ideas altered the way we interpret the natural world. Even today, we have Charles Darwin to thank for our understanding of biodiversity on Earth. More than 150 years after the publication of the *Origin of Species*, evolution by natural selection is still used to explain the many different species of plants and animals that exist today.

Timeline

1809
Charles Darwin is born on 12 February in Shrewsbury, England.

1817
Darwin attends a school in Shrewsbury run by George Case.
In the same year, his mother dies.

1818
Darwin attends Samuel Butler's school at Shrewsbury as a boarder – a student who lives at the school.

1825
Darwin is sent to the University of Edinburgh to study medicine.
The same year, the world's first public steam railway opens in England.

1828
Darwin goes to the University of Cambridge.

1831

Darwin is awarded a B.A. degree.

Later the same year, he is invited to join HMS *Beagle* as a naturalist for its survey voyage. He leaves with the *Beagle* on 27 December.

1832

The *Beagle* surveys the east coast of South America.

1833

Slavery is ended in the British Empire.

1834

The *Beagle* sails around the southern tip of South America into the Pacific Ocean.

Charles Babbage invents his 'analytical engine', a very early kind of computer.

1835

Darwin lives through an earthquake in Chile.

Later the same year, he reaches the Galapagos Islands.

1836

The *Beagle* finally returns to England on 2nd October.

1837

John Gould identifies Darwin's Galapagos birds as a new group of finch species. Darwin begins to wonder how they came to be different and draws his first evolutionary tree in his 'B' notebook.

Victoria becomes Queen of the United Kingdom of Great Britain and Ireland.

1838

Darwin reads an essay by Thomas Malthus that helps him to develop his theory of evolution by natural selection.

1839

Darwin marries his cousin, Emma Wedgwood. Later the same year, his first child, William Erasmus, is born.

1841

Darwin's second child, Anne Elizabeth, is born.

1842

Darwin moves to Down House in the village of Down, Kent.

His third child, Mary Eleanor, is born, but she lives for only three weeks.

1843

Darwin's fourth child, Henrietta Emma, known as Etty, is born.

1845

Darwin's fifth child, George Howard, is born.

1847

Darwin's sixth child, Elizabeth, known as Bessy, is born.

1848

Darwin's father dies and his seventh child, Francis, is born.

1850

Darwin's eighth child, Leonard, is born.

1851

Darwin's oldest daughter, Annie, dies aged ten, and his ninth child, Horace, is born.

1856

Darwin begins work on the book that will become the *Origin of Species*, and his tenth child, Charles Waring is born.

1858

Darwin receives a letter from Alfred Russel Wallace with an essay about species that is nearly the same as Darwin's own theory.

Darwin's youngest child, Charles Waring, dies of scarlet fever.

Darwin's and Wallace's theories of evolution are both read at a meeting of the Linnean Society.

1859

Darwin's book, *On the Origin of Species by means of Natural Selection*, is published while Darwin is recovering from one of his many attacks of illness.

1861

The American Civil War begins.

1862

Darwin grows a bushy beard to cover skin problems and avoid the pain of shaving.

1865

The American Civil War ends with a Union victory and the abolition of slavery in the United States. President Abraham Lincoln is assassinated.

1866

Alfred Nobel invents dynamite.

1869

The first US transcontinental railroad is completed.

1871

Darwin's second book is published: The *Descent of Man, and Selection in relation to Sex*.

1876

Darwin begins to write his life story for his family. Alexander Graham bell patents his invention, the telephone.

1879

Thomas Edison patents a practical electric light bulb.

1882

Darwin dies on 19 April, aged seventy-three, and is buried in Westminster Abbey.

Glossary

ape A creature that belongs to a group that includes orangutans, gorillas and chimpanzees. Humans are sometimes included in this group.

armadillo An insect-eating, nocturnal (active at night) mammal with strong claws for digging and an armour-like covering of bony plates.

atoll A ring-shaped coral reef.

bachelor A man who is not, and never has been, married.

bacteria Tiny single-celled organisms found everywhere on Earth that can only be seen using a microscope. They may be round, rod-shaped or spiral. Most bacteria are harmless to humans, but some can cause serious diseases including cholera, typhoid and plague.

botany The scientific study of plants.

Ceylon The island now known as Sri Lanka, located at the southern tip of India.

Chagas disease A disease spread by parasites on blood-sucking insects called kissing bugs in South and Central America.

consul An official chosen by a government to look after its citizens, trade and business in another country.

coral A rock-like substance formed from the skeletons of countless small marine creatures living together, forming a reef or island.

Crohn's Disease A medical condition that causes painful swelling of the lining of the gut.

dove A bird of the pigeon family, especially the smaller birds with pointed tails, sometimes pure white in colour.

eczema A medical condition that makes patches of skin rough, red, flaky and itchy.

elephantiasis A tropical disease caused by a worm-like parasite that makes a victim's arm, leg or other part of the body extremely swollen.

environment The natural surroundings including the soil, atmosphere, climate, plants and animals. The environment may mean the whole world or a small area.

equator An imaginary line around the middle of the Earth equally distant from the north and south poles.

essay A short piece of writing setting out the writer's views on a particular subject.

evolution The natural process responsible for producing plants and animals from older, simpler species.

extinct When a species of animal or plant has completely died out and no longer exists.

false keel An extra strip of timber fitted to the bottom of a ship's hull to protect the real keel from damage.

fertile A description of land, soil or water that is rich in food and so able to support healthy plant growth, and the animals that feed on the plants.

field trip A visit to a building or outdoors location for the purpose of studying something.

finch A small bird with short, strong beak for cracking seeds.

gaucho A South American word for someone skilled at riding horses.

genetic code The instructions within living cells that control how the cells grow and work.

geology The scientific study of the history of the planet Earth and its life, especially as they are recorded in rocks.

gross-bill A type of finch (bird) with a large beak. Also called a grosbeak.

hammock A bed made of fabric or rope mesh hanging from a rope at each end. Common on ships from the sixteenth century to the middle of the twentieth century.

iguana A large, plant-eating lizard with a spiny crest along its back, found mainly in South and Central America.

keel The part of a boat or ship that runs along the bottom of the hull from bow to stern.

knighthood An honour given by the king or queen to citizens of the United Kingdom who have done something very significant.

lagoon A stretch of water separated from the surrounding sea by rock, sandbanks or a coral reef.

lava Molten (liquid) rock flowing out of an erupting volcano.

Linnean Society A society that encourages the study of natural history and evolution.

lizard A type of reptile with a long body, four legs and rough, scaly skin.

Magellan Ferdinand Magellan (1480–1521), a skilled Portuguese explorer who led the first circumnavigation (round-the-world voyage).

Malay Archipelago Thousands of islands between southeast Asia and Australia, including Brunei, Singapore, East Malaysia, Indonesia, Java, Sumatra, the Philippines and East Timor.

mammal Any of a large group of warm-blooded animals that include humans. Mammals range in size from tiny bats the size of a bumble-bee to the biggest creature on Earth, the blue whale. Nearly all mammals give birth to live young.

mentor Someone who uses their wisdom and experience to give advice.

mockingbird A grey, long-tailed songbird that can mimic the songs of other birds.

mussel An edible freshwater or marine shellfish in a shell with two parts hinged on one side, enabling the shell to open for feeding and close.

naturalist Someone who studies the natural world.

natural selection The process by which some plants or animals are more likely than others to survive and produce young, because they are better suited to the conditions they live in. This is the process that drives evolution, gradually changing species so that they form new species.

orang-utan A large ape with long arms and red hair, from Borneo and Sumatra.

palpitation An unusually fast, strong or irregular heartbeat caused by stress, exercise or illness.

Patagonia A region at the southern end of South America, shared by Argentina and Chile.

Polynesia More than 1,000 islands in the central Pacific Ocean including Hawaii, Samoa, Tonga, Christmas Island and the Cook Islands.

Provisions Supplies of food, drink or equipment taken on a journey.

reptile Any of a large group of cold-blooded egg-laying animals that crawl on their belly or on legs, including snakes, lizards, crocodiles, turtles and tortoises.

schooner A sailing boat or ship with two or more masts, with the foremast (the mast at the front) shorter than the main-mast behind it.

scientific paper A report describing science research published in a science journal.

spa A place where water with minerals dissolved in it comes to the surface of the ground as a natural spring, where people go to improve their health.

species A group of plants or animals that are so similar to each other that they can breed with each other.

specimen An animal, plant or piece of rock collected as an example of its type.

St Elmo's fire A glow around sharp or pointed objects, caused by a strong electric field produced by, for example, a thunderstorm.

Strait of Magellan A natural channel between Tierra del Fuego and the South American mainland, through which ships can pass to travel between the Atlantic and Pacific oceans.

theory An idea or suggestion put forward to explain something.

Tierra del Fuego An island at the southern tip of South America.

trade wind One of the winds that blow almost constantly in one direction. They are called trade winds because they have been used by sailing ships for centuries to cross the Atlantic and Pacific oceans.

transmutation Changing something, such as a species, from one form to a different form.

vertebrate Any animal that has a backbone.

water cure Using water, especially mineral water, to improve health by drinking the water and bathing in it. Also known as hydrotherapy.

yard A pole fixed horizontally across a ship's mast so that a sail can be hung from it.

yardarm The tapered end of a ship's yard.

zoology The scientific study of animals and their behaviour, anatomy (bodily structure), habitats (where they live) and evolution.

Index